I Am Not Afraid

I Am
Not
Afraid

Arlynn President

Dedication

This book is dedicated to my son, my firstborn and miracle child, Elioenai. You are a resilient, brave, unwavering, and strong man of God.

Arlynn President

Mom!" Eli cried out in terror, tears filling his eyes. It was now the third night in a row that he heard noises in his closet and under his bed. He just could not understand why this was happening, since his parents taught him to pray every night before going to sleep and they would do this together.

"There's a monster under my bed and something in my room and I don't know what else to do," Eli thought as he pulled the covers over himself. Fear fell heavily over him like a ton of bricks, and he began to sweat profusely and tremble until he finally fell asleep.

In the morning, when he awoke, he felt defeated and discouraged. Eli did not get much sleep last night, once again. As he did his morning routine of getting dressed and brushing his teeth, he noticed the bags under his eyes in the mirror and sighed.

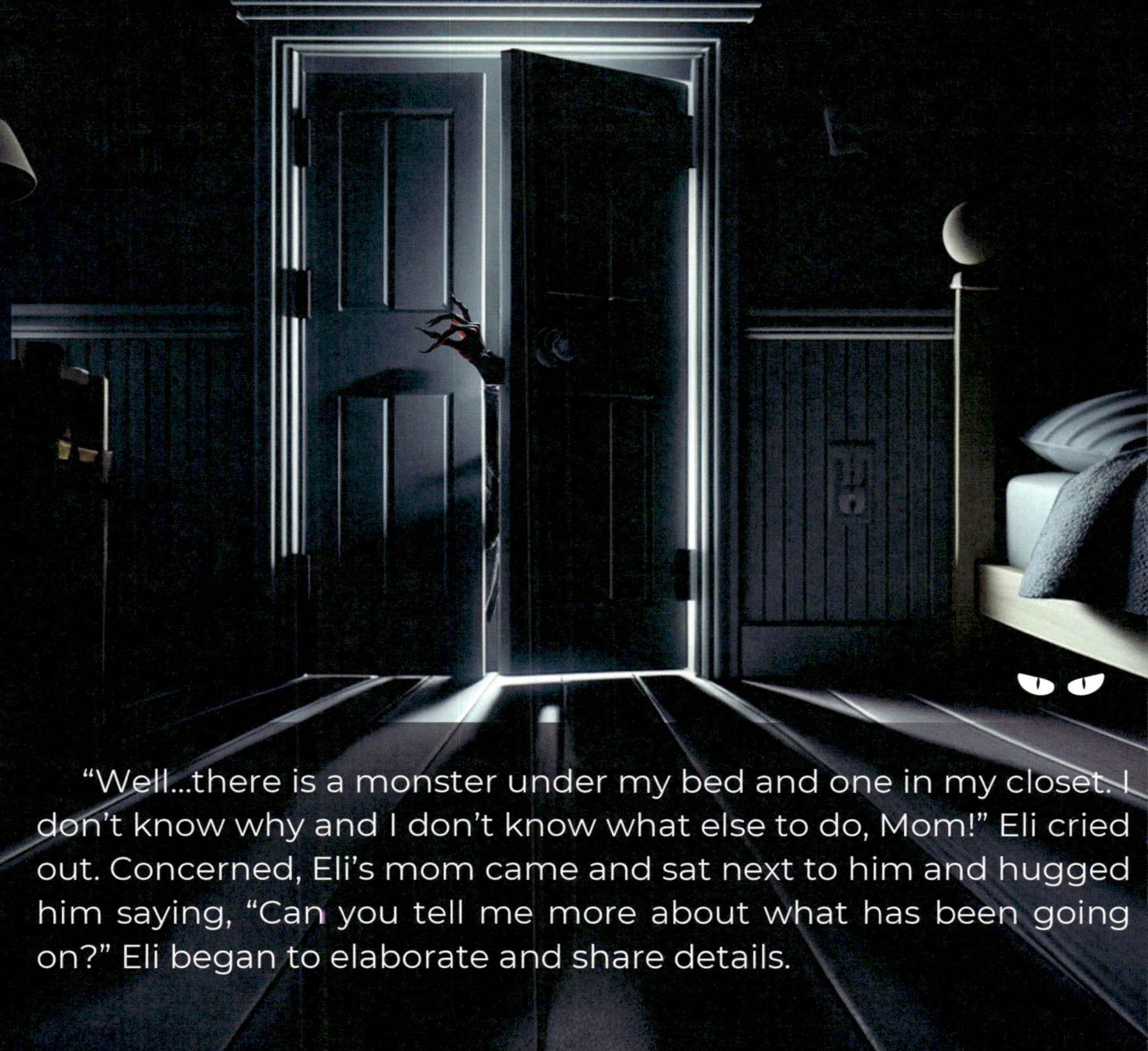

"Well...there is a monster under my bed and one in my closet. I don't know why and I don't know what else to do, Mom!" Eli cried out. Concerned, Eli's mom came and sat next to him and hugged him saying, "Can you tell me more about what has been going on?" Eli began to elaborate and share details.

He came downstairs and sat at the table while his mom finished making breakfast. "Good morning sunshine, how'd you sleep?" Eli's mom asked. Eli let out a huge sigh and very weakly said "Not good." She turned around and asked, "Why?" "Mom, can I tell you something?" he asked. "Of course honey," she replied. "I feel a little embarrassed...," Eli muttered. "You can trust me. Go ahead and tell me, baby," his mom said.

"Mom, I hear someone walking in my room at nighttime and there's no one there, but I can hear them!" he exclaimed.

"The monster in my closet tries to open the closet door, and I can hear it growl! And the monster under my bed pulls my covers off and sometimes comes up to sit by me on my bed.

I feel so scared! I don't know why they keep scaring me if we pray together every night for Jesus to keep us safe."

Eli's mom could see the fear in his eyes. The Lord prompted her to speak life into Eli at this very moment and to have a teaching moment for how to handle these types of situations. "Honey, I am so sorry you've been going through that," she said as she pulled Eli in for a hug.

"Jesus has been with you all along, and He has not left you. I understand that you feel scared, but did you know that Jesus Christ gave us power and dominion over all power of the enemy and nothing shall hurt us? *(Luke 10:19 'Behold I give you the authority to trample upon serpents and scorpions (demons/unclean spirits) and over all power of the enemy, and nothing shall by any means hurt you.)*

I want you to remember these 3 things I'm about to tell you, if that monster comes back to bother you, okay?" Eli lifted his head up and gazed into his mothers eyes and replied, "Okay mommy."

"Okay, so these 3 things you are to say to those monsters when you feel afraid:

1. In Jesus name, get out of my room and leave me alone!
2. I bind and rebuke every demonic spirit and command you to go to the feet of Jesus and never come back in Jesus name
3. I cancel your assignment in Jesus name

Eli repeated after his mother and he began to feel confident. It was in this very moment that Eli was introduced to spiritual warfare and he was taught how to fight the enemy back. Eli's mother held his hand and took him around the house and continued praying out loud, commanding all demonic and unclean spirits to leave the house in Jesus name. She taught Eli how to anoint the house with oil, and they anointed every room that day. "I can feel God's peace, Mommy!" exclaimed Eli.

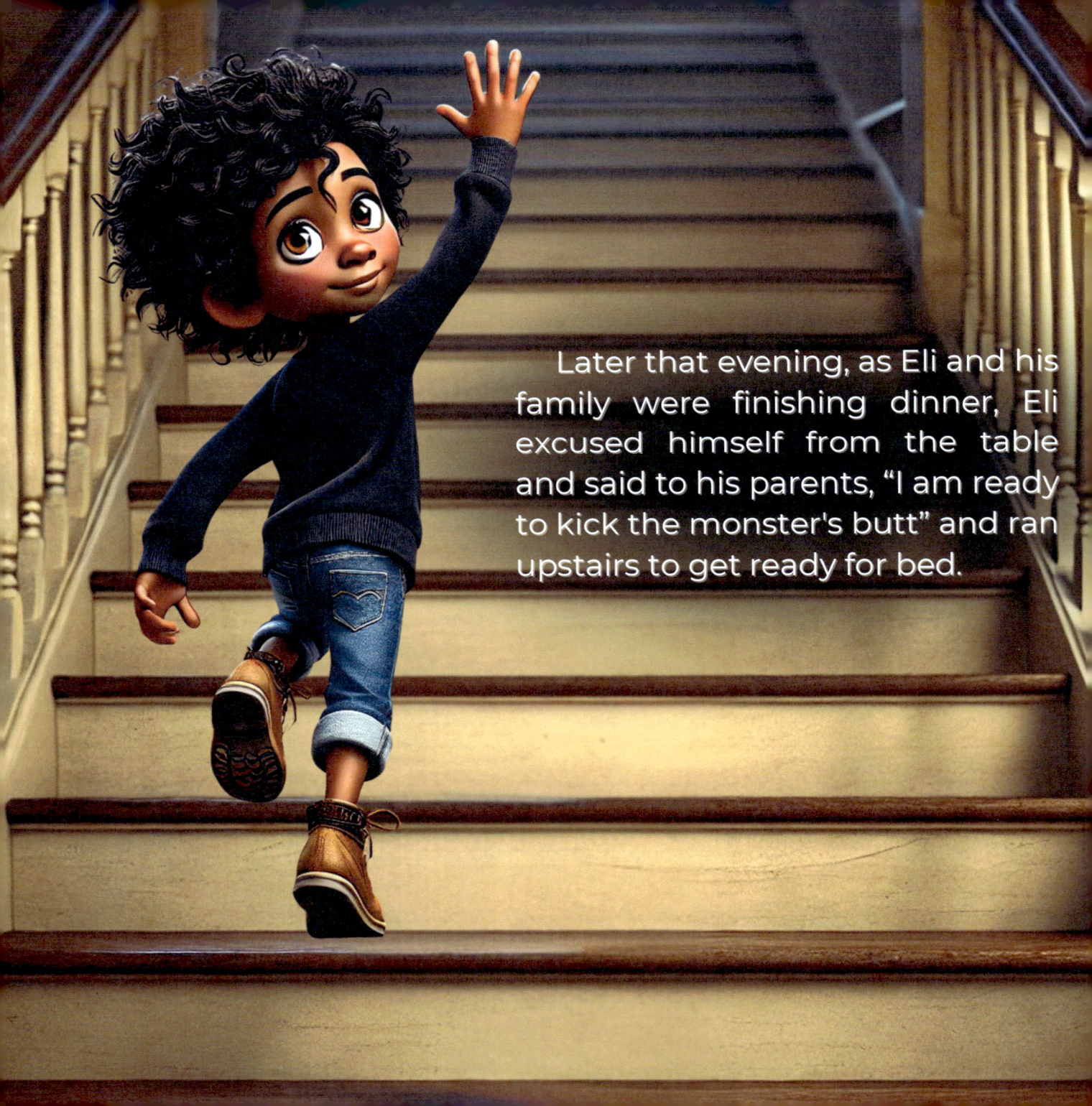

Later that evening, as Eli and his family were finishing dinner, Eli excused himself from the table and said to his parents, "I am ready to kick the monster's butt" and ran upstairs to get ready for bed.

He brushed his teeth while his mother waited for him in his bed to tuck him in and pray together. He came in smiling ear to ear and said, "I am not afraid Mommy. Thank you for teaching me how to fight those monsters."

She kissed him goodnight on the forehead and said, "Remember, you have the power and authority over these monsters, in the name of Jesus," and walked out and closed the door.

Later that night while everyone was asleep, just as Eli had suspected, he heard the noise under his bed. It was breathing heavily. Next, he heard something moving in his closet and could hear a low growl. The door creaked and suddenly the atmosphere felt heavy.

Eli sat up, and at first, he closed his eyes. However, he remembered that he did not have to be afraid. This night was the night he would face his fears.

He confronted the monsters and commanded them to leave in the name of Jesus. Eli opened up his mouth and said "I command you to get out of my room in Jesus name, leave me alone!" at first, it seemed nothing had changed, the monsters were still growling and trying to intimidate Eli.

I bind and rebuke you in Jesus' name, go to the feet of Jesus and never come back. Go in Jesus' name!" Suddenly, Eli could feel a peace come over him and the noise was less. "I cancel your assignment in Jesus' name!" Eli proclaimed, "Jesus is here with me and you can't be here, leave me alone. Go in Jesus' name," and it was done. Just like that, the room fell silent and God's peace overwhelmed Eli's room.

He saw angels of the Lord in the room with him, and they were wearing armor, like a knight, standing tall. They dragged the monsters out of his room. One of the angels said to Eli, "Your Father in heaven is very proud of you, for He has given you the power to trample over darkness. You put your authority and faith to work, and this pleases the Lord." Eli continued to feel an overwhelming peace flood into his room, one that he had never felt before, a peace that passes all understanding.

Eli slept in the Lord's presence from that night on. He went on to testify to his family, friends in his neighborhood, and friends at church, of what God did for him. "If He did it for me, He can do it for you," he told his friends, who were going through a similar situation. "God is love, and perfect love casts out all fear, we don't have to be afraid." He encouraged those around him to pray and taught them how to command Satan and his demons to leave them alone in the name of Jesus. "I am not afraid," exclaimed Eli, "God is with me."

THE END

FOR THE READER....

If you are experiencing something like what Eli experienced, know that you too have the power and authority to trample over darkness and command demonic spirits to leave you alone in the name of Jesus.

Pray with me,

"Dear God,

I thank You for being with me always, and because of that I do not have to be afraid. I don't have to be afraid because you have not given me a spirit of fear, but of love, power, and a sound mind. Your Word says that no weapon formed against me shall prosper, and I receive it in Jesus name. I have the authority that Jesus has given me through His Holy Spirit and now I bind and rebuke every demonic spirit that is against me and I command you to go to the abyss now in Jesus name.

I cancel every demonic assignment over my life, over my health, my family, and my home in Jesus name. Lord, I ask that You would send Your warrior angels to dismantle the kingdom of darkness and arrest the enemy in Jesus name, and I ask for Your protection in Jesus name. Thank You heavenly Father for fighting my battles. In You I will rest knowing that I do not have to worry or be afraid because You are in control. In Jesus name, I pray, amen."

A verse to declare over yourself before going to sleep:

Psalms 4:8
"I will both lie down in peace, and sleep; for You alone, O Lord, make me dwell in safety."

Verses to Remember
- *No weapon formed against me shall prosper, and every tongue that rises against me in judgment I condemn. (Isaiah 54:17)*
- *Perfect love casts out all fear (1 John 4:18)*
- *Behold I give you the authority to trample upon serpents and scorpions (demons/unclean spirits) and over all power of the enemy, and nothing shall by any means hurt you (Luke 10:19)*
- *I do not have the spirit of fear but of power, love, and a sound mind. (2 Tim. 1:7)*
- *I overcome all because greater is He that is within me than he that is in the world. (1 John 4:4)*

About Arlynn President

Arlynn President is a lover of Jesus Christ, a wife, mother, worshipper, minister, and author. Arlynn President ministers alongside her husband, Neil President, through their ministry Kingdom Lifestyle Ministries, where they dedicate themselves to preaching the Gospel, winning souls for the Kingdom of God, and equipping believers through worship, teaching, and deliverance, to live a Holy Spirit-filled life for the glory of God.

Both Neil and Arlynn President take great joy in ministering to those who are spiritually hungry for God and are seeking out the deeper things of God. Arlynn President has ministered and served in various churches as worship director, worship leader, and teacher, building up worship teams, mentoring people, and teaching them how to cultivate a relationship with Jesus. She is recognized as a servant leader, and known for her kindness, compassion, and servant heart which overflows with the manifestation of God's love.

Arlynn President is a mother to Elioenai (a promise of the Lord), and as a woman of faith, Arlynn has been used by the Holy Spirit to speak life into other women and mothers and empower them to live out all that God has for them. She also has a love for children. Having taught in schools for a few years, the Lord is using all of her experiences to pour into her little one, and many other children through her books.

Along with ministerial responsibilities, Arlynn considers her first ministry to be her family. This includes her husband Neil, and her son Elioenai.

MORE INFORMATION

To learn more about Kingdom Lifestyle Ministries, make sure to scan the QR code below.

Made in United States
Troutdale, OR
12/05/2024